AF322881

The 17:18 Series

The Book of Exodus Chapters 1–21

Joel R. Beeke and Rob Wynalda

This book belongs to:

____

Given by: _______________________

Date: __________________________

Published by
Reformation Heritage Books
2965 Leonard St. NE
Grand Rapids, MI 49525
616-977-0889 / Fax 616-285-3246
e-mail: orders@heritagebooks.org
website: www.heritagebooks.org

ISBN 978-1-60178-551-0

Cover Design: Bethany Sanderson and Steve Coy
Journible® Design: Rob Wynalda

Why the 17:18 series?

In Deuteronomy 17, Moses is leaving final instructions concerning the future of Israel. As a prophet of God, Moses foretells of when Israel will place a king over the nation (v. 14). In verses 16 & 17, he lists items that the king could not do as king. In verse 18, he transitions to what he should do as king.

The king is commanded not to simply acquire a copy of the law (the entire book of Deuteronomy) from the "scroll publishing house," but to handwrite his own copy of the law. The purpose of such a copy written by his own hand was so that:

* he would read it
* he would learn to fear the Lord
* he would obey the commands of God
* his heart would not become proud
* he would not turn to the right or the left from following the law (Prov. 4:27)
* also, his sons would serve in the kingdom after him (Deut. 17:19, 20).

Thirty-four hundred years later, educators are "discovering" that students who physically write out their notes by hand have a much greater retention rate than those who simply hear or visually read the information. Apparently, God knew this to be true for the kings of Israel also.

From such understanding came the conception of this series of books.

Have a great time writing and learning the Word of God,

Rob Wynalda
Romans 1:16

The Purpose of the Journible®

Engagement:

The Journible® is a profoundly simple attempt to aid a person's ability to engage the Word of God by slowing down the process of simply reading the text. The book is organized so that the "scribe" can slowly and thoughtfully engage the text while leaving plenty of room to write comments and questions about the text (Deuteronomy 17:18; Psalm 119; 2 Timothy 3:16, 17).

Legacy:

Journibles® provide a legacy to pass on from one generation to the next. The Journible® creates an opportunity for one generation to communicate in writing to the next generation their insights and personal applications of the text (Deuteronomy 6).

How to use this book

This book is organized so that the scribe (you) will handwrite your very own copy of Exodus. You will be writing the text of the Bible only on the right-hand page of the book. This should make for easier writing and also allows ample space on the left page of your open text to write your own notes and comments. From time to time a question or word will be lightly printed on the left page; these questions are to aid in further study, but should not interfere with your own notes and comments. This means that you are encouraged not only to write your own "copy" of the Bible, but also to write your own notes concerning the text.

Yes, we are setting aside our mass-produced Gutenberg Bibles and attempting to get back to the simple handwritten copy of the text.

Notes

(1–4) How does this genealogy connect Exodus with Genesis?

(5) What was Joseph's status in Egypt? See Genesis 41:40 and 47:25.

(7) Why is their growth significant? See Genesis 12:2.

(9–11) How did the affliction of God's people relate to God's providence and plan? See Genesis 15:13 and Psalm 105:25.

Exodus 1:1-9

1

2

3

4

5

6

7

8

9

Notes

(12) How does this illustrate the power of God in persecution?

(15–16) After propaganda (v. 10) and oppression (v. 11) failed, what did the king command? What would this likely do to Israel over time?

10

11

12

13

14

15

Notes

(17) What motivated the midwives to disobey the king of Egypt?

(20–21) What did God do after the midwives' civil disobedience?

16

17

18

19

20

21

Notes

(22) How did Pharaoh respond to the failure of his plan with the midwives?

22

Notes

(2) What do we see about Moses's parents? See Hebrews 11:23.

(3) How do the actions of Moses's mother express faith in God?

(5–6) What would you expect to happen to a baby in the Nile? What amazing result came from putting the baby in the Nile?

Exodus 2:1-6

1

2

3

4

5

6

Notes

(8–10) What is ironic about this scene? How does it display God's wise providence?

(11–12) What motivated Moses to do this? See Acts 7:23–25 and Hebrews 11:24–26.

7

8

9

10

11

12

Notes

(14) What was the attitude of the Hebrew man toward Moses? What does his attitude show us about sinful men's hearts toward God's servants and toward Christ Himself? See Acts 7:35–37.

(16–17) Compare Moses to Jacob. See Genesis 29:10.

13

14

15

16

17

18

Notes

(19) How does this show us Moses's character?

(22) What did Moses name his son? Why?

(24–25) What does it mean that God remembered (see Gen. 8:1), and what does it reveal about Him?

19

20

21

22

23

24

25

Notes

(2) Who was in the bush? What might fire signify? See Exodus 13:21; 19:18; and 24:17.

(4) Who was in the bush now? What does that imply about the angel of the Lord (v. 2)?

Exodus 3:1-5

1

2

3

4

5

Notes

(6) Who is this God? What does "God of" imply? See Genesis 17:7–8.

(7–9) What does this teach us about God and prayer?

(10) What did God call Moses to do?

Exodus 3:6-10

6

7

8

9

10

Notes

(11–12) What was Moses's first objection? How did God answer it?

(13–14) What was Moses's second objection? How did God answer it? What might God's name "I AM" mean? See Revelation 1:8.

Exodus 3:11-15

11

12

13

14

15

Notes

(17) To whom did God first promise the land of the Canaanites?
See Genesis 15:18–21.

(19–20) What did the Lord predict about Egypt and its king?

(21–22) What did God promise about Israel's departure?
See Genesis 15:14.

16

17

18

19

20

21

Notes

22

Notes

(1–9) What was Moses's third objection? What does it show us about Moses that he kept raising objections against God's calling on him? How did God answer this objection?

(5) What is one purpose of miracles?

Exodus 4:1-6

2

3

4

5

6

Notes

(10–12) What was Moses's fourth objection? How did God answer it?

7

8

9

10

11

12

Notes

(13–14) Why did God's anger burn against Moses? What does this teach us?

(15–16) How did the relationship between Moses and Aaron picture the relationship between God and His prophet?

(18) How did Moses honor his father-in-law?

13

14

15

16

17

18

Notes

(21) What was the ultimate reason Pharaoh would not let Israel go?

(22–23) What did the Lord call Israel?

19

20

21

22

23

24

Notes

(25–26) Why is it surprising that Moses had not circumcised his son? See Genesis 17:9–14.

(31) How did the people respond to the word and miracles of the Lord?

25

26

27

28

29

30

31

Notes

(1) What did the Lord call Israel, and why?

(2) How did Pharaoh reply? What did that reveal about him?

(6–9) What was Pharaoh's response to God's request?

Exodus 5:1-6

1

2

3

4

5

6

Notes

(10–14) How did God's word make things worse for Israel?

7

8

9

10

11

12

13

Notes

(15–21) How did Pharaoh's tactic cleverly turn Israel against Moses?

4

5

6

7

8

9

Notes

(22–23) How did Moses react? What lessons can we learn about patience from this?

20

21

22

23

Notes

(1) How did Pharaoh's disobedience set the stage for God to glorify Himself?

(2–8) How many times does God say, "I am the Lord" in this text? Why?

(4, 8) What ancient promise stands behind God's saving work in Exodus?

(6) What did God promise to do for them in Egypt? (This summarizes chapters 1–18.)

Exodus 6:1-6

2

3

4

5

6

Notes

(7) What did God promise to do afterward? (This summarizes chapters 19–40.)

(9) How did Israel respond to these promises? Why?

(12) How did Moses describe his lips? What does that mean? See Leviticus 26:40–41 and Deuteronomy 10:16.

7

8

9

10

11

12

Notes

(14–25) Genealogies often introduce important people in the Bible. Whom does this genealogy introduce? What does their family history suggest about them?

3

4

5

6

7

8

Notes

19

20

21

22

23

24

25

Notes

(28–30) How do these verses compare to verses 10–13?

Exodus 6:26-30

26

27

28

29

30

Notes

(1–2) How did Moses act like God, and Aaron like God's prophet?

(3–5) Why did God harden Pharaoh's heart?

(6) How did Moses and Aaron respond to God's commission?

Exodus 7:1-7

2

3

4

5

6

7

Notes

(10) Pharaoh wore a headdress with an erect cobra symbolizing his patron goddess. What, then, might it mean that God chose to do this miracle?

(12) How does this show the power and limitations of the devil's servants?

(13) Why did Pharaoh refuse to listen to Moses and Aaron?

8

9

10

11

12

13

14

Notes

(17) What was the first plague on Egypt? What was its purpose?

15

16

17

18

19

Notes

(20) Why was it a sign of divine justice to turn the river to blood? See Exodus 1:22 and Revelation 16:5–6.

(21) The economy and very life of the Egyptians depended on the Nile, which they viewed as a gift from their gods. How would this plague affect the nation?

20

21

22

23

24

25

Notes

(1–3) What was the second plague?

(5) By what means did God send the plagues?

Exodus 8:1-7

1

2

3

4

5

6

7

Notes

(8) How did Pharaoh respond to this plague?

(10) What is the purpose of this plague and its removal?

(12) What role did Moses play in this plague's removal?

Exodus 8:8-12

8

9

10

11

12

Notes

(15) Why did Pharaoh harden his heart? What does this teach us about sinners and their prayers and promises to God?

(16–17) What was the third plague? What is missing that was present in the first two?

(18–19) What is God's "finger" (see Ps. 8:3; Luke 11:20)? What does this event teach us about the Lord in comparison to the gods of this world?

Exodus 8:13-18

13

14

15

16

17

18

Notes

(21) What was the fourth plague?

(22) What was the purpose of this plague?

(23) Why did the plague not come on Israel? The word "division" or "distinction" or "difference" is literally "redemption" (Ps. 130:7). What might this imply?

19

20

21

22

23

Notes

(25-28) What is wrong with Pharaoh's permission? How might this have tempted Moses?

(29–31) Why did God remove the plague? How is this a picture of Christ?

24

25

26

27

28

29

Notes

30

31

32

Notes

(2–3) What was the fifth plague?

(4, 6–7) How did this plague affect Israel?

Exodus 9:1-6

2

3

4

5

6

Notes

(8–10) What was the sixth plague? How is this plague different from the fourth and fifth?

(11) How did this plague affect the sorcerers?

(12) Why did Pharaoh continue to resist God?

7

8

9

10

11

12

Notes

(14–16) What was God's intention in the plagues?

(18) What was the seventh plague?

13

14

15

16

17

18

Notes

(19–20) How did God show mercy during the seventh plague?

19

20

21

22

23

Notes

(24) How did this plague show the power of God?

(27) What did Pharaoh confess?

(29) What was the purpose of God's removing this plague?

24

25

26

27

28

29

Notes

(34) Was Pharaoh sinning when he hardened his heart?

30

31

32

33

34

35

Notes

(1–2) Though Pharaoh sinned in hardening his heart (9:34), what ultimate explanation did the Lord give for why it happened?

(3) What does this question imply about Pharaoh?

(4–6) What was the eighth plague?

Exodus 10:1-5

2

3

4

5

Notes

(10–11) What compromise did Pharaoh offer them?

Exodus 10:6-10

6

7

8

9

10

Notes

(14–15) How devastating was this plague?

11

12

13

14

15

Notes

(16–17) How is Pharaoh an example of false repentance?

(19) How did God demonstrate His complete control over the locusts?

(21) What was the ninth plague? How is this plague like the third and sixth, but unlike the others?

(22–23) What does darkness signify? See Joel 2:1–2; Zephaniah 1:15; and Matthew 27:45–46.

Exodus 10:16-22

16

17

18

19

20

21

22

Notes

(24–26) What final compromise did Pharaoh propose? Why was it necessary that Israel leave not one animal behind?

(29) What did Moses predict?

23

24

25

26

27

28

29

Notes

(1–3) How did this show that events happen as God decreed? See Exodus 3:21–22.

(4–6) What was the tenth plague? How was it a just judgment? See Exodus 1:22 and 4:22–23.

Exodus 11:1-6

1

2

3

4

5

6

Notes

(7) How did this plague affect Israel? What did this show?

(9–10) Why did Pharaoh not listen to Moses?

7

8

9

10

Notes

(1–2) What place did God assign that month in the Hebrew calendar? What might that suggest?

(3–5) What must every family in Israel take? Why unblemished? See Leviticus 1:3 and 1 Peter 1:19.

(6–8) What must each household do with it?

Exodus 12:1-6

2

3

4

5

6

Notes

(11) How must Israel eat it?

(12–13) Why is this festival called Passover? How did the blood of the lamb save Israel? How did it point to Christ? See John 1:29 and Revelation 5:6, 9–10.

Exodus 12:7-12

7

8

9

10

11

12

Notes

(15–20) What feast immediately followed the Passover? What did leaven represent? See Exodus 23:18; 34:25; Luke 12:1; and 1 Corinthians 5:6–8?

13

14

15

16

17

Notes

(22) How is this a picture of faith in Christ?

18

19

20

21

22

23

Notes

(26–27) What did God command about the children?

(29–30) How extensive was God's judgment?

24

25

26

27

28

29

Notes

(35–36) How did God's promise come true? See Exodus 11:1–3.

30

31

32

33

34

35

Notes

(37) How many men were in Israel? See Exodus 38:26.

(39) Why did they bake unleavened bread?

(40) How long was Israel in Egypt?

36

37

38

39

40

41

Notes

(43–49) Who may eat the Passover?

(46) What did the Lord command about the lamb's bones? How did that foreshadow Christ? See John 19:31–37.

42

43

44

45

46

47

48

Notes

(50) How did Israel respond to these ceremonial laws of God?

Exodus 12:49-51

49

50

51

Notes

(1–2) What did God say about all the firstborn?

(3) What did the Lord command about that day? Why was that important for Israel to do? How do Christians do that today regarding their redemption in Christ?

2

3

4

5

6

Notes

(8) What was required of parents?

(11–16) Why did God claim the firstborn males?

7

8

9

10

11

12

Notes

(17) Why did God not send Israel to Canaan by the most direct route?

13

14

15

16

17

Notes

(19) Why did Moses take Joseph's bones (see Gen. 50:24–25)? How is that a testimony to God's faithfulness over the centuries?

(21–22) How did God manifest His presence with Israel in the wilderness? What did that do for them? How might it have affected them? See Nehemiah 9:12, 19.

18

19

20

21

22

Notes

(2–3) Where did the Lord lead Israel?

(4) Why did Pharaoh pursue Israel?

(7) Chariots were fast and powerful machines of war that carried deadly archers. How would it have affected the former slaves of Pharaoh to see him coming with hundreds of chariots?

Exodus 14:1-7

1

2

3

4

5

6

7

Notes

(11–12) What does Israel's response reveal about them?

8

9

10

11

12

Notes

(13–14) What did Moses command Israel? Why? How does this illustrate saving faith?

(17–18) What was God's purpose in staging and winning this battle?

Exodus 14:13-18

13

14

15

16

17

18

Notes

(19) Who was with Israel in the cloud? Who is that? See Exodus 3:2–4.

(22) What did this require of Israel (see Heb. 11:29)? Why is this event plainly a miracle and not a natural event?

19

20

21

22

23

Notes

(24–25) How did the Lord terrify the Egyptians?
See Psalm 77:16–20.

(28) How did the Lord show His total sovereignty over His enemies?

24

25

26

27

28

Notes

(30) What did the Lord do for Israel on that day? What does this foreshadow?

(31) How did Israel respond to the Lord's mighty work?

Exodus 14:29-31

29

30

31

Notes

(1) How did Moses lead Israel to respond to their salvation?

(2–3) What did they say about the Lord in their praises?

(6–7) What two attributes of God did His salvation display?

Exodus 15:1-7

1

2

3

4

5

6

7

Notes

(9) How did the enemies of God show their arrogance?

(11) What third attribute of God did His salvation reveal?

(13) What is the fourth attribute of God celebrated here?

(14–16) How did the news of God's victory affect the nations of Canaan?

Exodus 15:8-14

8

9

10

11

12

13

14

Notes

(18) How did Moses sum up this song of salvation?

15

16

17

18

19

20

Notes

(22) What situation did Israel find itself in three days later? Why was that serious?

(25–26) How did God show His care for Israel in the wilderness? How did He test them?

21

22

23

24

25

26

Notes

27

Notes

(1) How long has it been since the exodus?

(2–3) What does this grumbling reveal about the people? What does it show about their faith at the Red Sea? See Exodus 14:31.

(4) Why do you think God was giving Israel only enough food for one day?

Exodus 16:1-5

2

3

4

5

Notes

(6–12) How many times does "the LORD" appear in these verses? How does this relate to God's purpose in these events (vv. 6, 12)?

(8) When they grumbled against God's messengers, against whom did they grumble?

6

7

8

9

10

11

Notes

(12) How does this verse demonstrate God's grace to sinners?

(15) What was manna like? See also verse 31.

(17–18) How much manna did God supply? What lesson was He teaching?

12

13

14

15

16

17

Notes

(22–26) What did God do to restore Israel to keeping the Sabbath? How does this show that keeping the Sabbath requires faith?

8

9

0

1

2

3

Notes

(27–28) What did people do on the Sabbath? What does this reveal about their hearts?

24

25

26

27

28

29

30

Notes

(32–34) What did God tell them to do with a sample of the manna? Why? On "the testimony," see Exodus 25:16 and 31:18.

(35) How was the manna a reminder of God's faithfulness? See Joshua 5:11–12.

31

32

33

34

35

36

Notes

(1) What trial did Israel experience?

(3) Of what did Israel accuse Moses? What were they saying about God's character?

(5) What had Moses done with this rod in the past?

Exodus 17:1-5

Notes

(6) Who deserved to be struck with the rod? What did Moses strike at God's command? What did it represent? See Deuteronomy 32:4; Psalm 78:15, 20, 35; and 1 Corinthians 10:4.

(8) Who is Amalek? What did they do? See Genesis 36:12 and Deuteronomy 25:17–18.

(9) This is the first mention of Joshua in the Bible. What did he do here?

(11–13) Upon what did Israel's victory depend? What did Aaron and Hur do? How does this show Moses's inadequacy and point us beyond him to Christ?

Exodus 17:6-11

6

7

8

9

10

11

Notes

(15) Moses named the altar "the LORD is my banner" (Jehovahnissi). What does that mean in this context?

2

3

4

5

6

Notes

(1) What prompted Jethro to visit Moses?

(4) Why did Moses name his second son Eliezer?

Exodus 18:1-6

Notes

(7) How did Moses honor his father-in-law?

(9–11) How did the story of God's works for Israel affect Jethro? What does this show us about God's purposes for His works of salvation? See Exodus 9:16 and Psalm 98:2–3

7

8

9

10

11

Notes

(13–18) What was "not good" about what Moses was doing?

12

13

14

15

16

17

Notes

(19–23) What solution did Jethro propose?

(21) What are the qualifications for leaders? Why are these qualifications important?

18

19

20

21

22

Notes

(24) Consider who Moses was and what he had done during the exodus. How does Moses's response to his father-in-law show his humility?

23

24

25

26

27

Notes

(1–2) Where was Israel at this point in its journey? Why is that important? See Exodus 3:12.

(3) What function did Moses perform?

(4) Of what did the Lord remind Israel? What do "eagles' wings" represent? See Deuteronomy 32:11–12 and Isaiah 40:31.

(5–6) What did the Lord promise Israel? What is the significance of the word "if"?

Exodus 19:1-6

1

2

3

4

5

6

Notes

(7–8) What function did Moses perform here?

(9) Why did God come in a cloud?

(11–13) What was God showing Israel about His presence?

7

8

9

10

11

12

Notes

(16–19) How did the Lord make Himself known at Mount Sinai? What would this have communicated to Israel? How did this prefigure judgment day? See Revelation 11:17–19.

13

14

15

16

17

18

Notes

(22) Why is the mountain so dangerous?

19

20

21

22

23

24

25

Notes

(1–2) How did the Lord introduce the Ten Commandments?

(3) How might people break the first commandment in a secular society?

(4–6) What did God forbid in the second commandment? What motives did He give?

(7) What is God's name? Why is it offensive to God to treat His name as "vain," or worthless?

(8–11) What is the fourth commandment? What is its basis?

Exodus 20:1-8

1

2

3

4

5

6

7

8

Notes

(12–17) If the Lord is the focus of the first four commandments, what is the focus of the next six? What areas of life do they regulate?

(17) How does the tenth commandment teach us that God's laws are not just about behavior?

9

10

11

12

13

14

15

16

17

Notes

(19) What did God's glory provoke Israel to desire?

(20) How could Moses tell them not to fear, but then commend fear?

18

19

20

21

22

23

Notes

(25) What was the danger of artistically shaping the stones of an altar? See verse 4.

24

25

26

Notes

(2) How did God limit slavery among the Hebrews?

(7–11) How did God protect female slaves?

1

2

3

4

5

6

7

Notes

(12–14) How did God distinguish between murder and accidental killing?

8

9

10

11

12

13

14

Notes

(15, 17) What penalty did striking or cursing parents receive?

(16) What does this law imply about slave trade (human trafficking)?

(20) What happened to the master if his slave died from his abuse?

15

16

17

18

19

20

21

Notes

(22–23) What penalty was inflicted for causing premature birth, even if the child was healthy? What if the child died?

(24–25) In this context, does this principle speak to personal revenge or judicial punishment?

(26–27) What happened to the master if he caused his slave permanent injury? How does this law clarify the application of verses 24 and 25?

(28–36) How did God teach Israel about the principle of liability for negligence?

22

23

24

25

26

27

28

Notes

(30) Explain the ransom. How did it foreshadow Christ? See Mark 10:45.

29

30

31

32

33

34

Notes

35

36

Notes

Notes

Notes

Notes

Notes

Notes

Notes

Notes

Notes

Notes

Notes

Notes